08 07 06 05 04 03 02   10 9 8 7 6 5 4 3 2 1

I love
to see
the
temple.

I'm going there someday.

T_o *feel the Holy Spirit,*

T_o
*listen
and
to pray.*

For the temple is a house of God,

A *place of love and beauty.*

I'll prepare myself while I am young;

T his is my sacred duty.

I love
to see
the
temple.

I'll go inside someday.

I'll covenant with my Father;

I'll promise to obey.

For the temple is a holy place where we are sealed together.

As a child of God, I've learned this truth: A family is forever.